W9-CJO-404

Origami
Paper Airplanes

Didier Boursin

FIREFLY BOOKS

A FIREFLY BOOK

Published by Firefly Books Ltd. 2001

First Printing 2001

U.S. Cataloging-in-Publication Data
   (Library of Congress Standards)

Boursin, Didier.
    Origami airplanes / Didier Boursin. –1st ed.
[64] p.: col. ill.; cm.
Summary: 28 origami designs of aircraft and flying objects.
ISBN: 1-55209-616-5 (paper)
ISBN: 1-55209-626-2 (bound)
1. Origami. 2. Paper airplanes. 3. Paper work. I. Title.
745.592   21   2001

Published in the United States in 2001 by
Firefly Books (U.S.) Inc.
P.O. Box 1338, Ellicott Station
Buffalo, New York, 14205

National Library of Canada Cataloguing Publication Data

Boursin, Didier
    Origami airplanes

ISBN: 1-55209-616-5 (paper)
ISBN: 1-55209-626-2 (bound)

1. Origami–Juvenile literature. 2. Paper airplanes–Juvenile literature.
I. Title.

TT870.B682 2001   j745.592   C2001-930720-9

Published in Canada in 2001 by
Firefly Books Ltd.
3680 Victoria Park Ave.
Willowdale, Ontario
M2H 3K1

Photography: Cactus Studio–Fabrice Besse
Photo Styling: Didier Boursin and Sonia Roy
Black and white photo (p.4): Guillaume and Angelo photo by Didier Boursin
Graphic Design (cover, interior design, diagrams): Nicolas Piroux
Editor: Youna Duhamel
Editorial Director: Catherine Franck-Dandres
Technical co-ordination: Nicolas Perrier
Photoengraving: Nord Compo
Translation and Origami consultation: John Reid

Printed and bound in Canada by Friesens, Altona, Manitoba

Acknowledgments

I wanted this work to be a meeting of creators from the four corners of the world because paper-folding is an international language. I thank those creators who have demonstrated their friendship by trusting me with their models.

For France: Michel Roy and Nicolas Beaudiez
For the United States: Stephen Weiss
For Japan: Takeshi Inoué
Thanks to Setsuko for advice.
Thanks to Fabrice Besse, my accomplice, for his photos.

I also wish to thank all those who, from near or far, have encouraged me in my venture: Paul Jackson, Nick Robinson, Steve and Megumi Biddle (Great Britain), Robert Noale (United States), Tomonao Hayashi, Koryo Miura and Hodi Husimi (Japan), Carlos Pomaron (Spain), Lionel Albertino, Sonia Roy (France).

You may send your comments and personal experiences to me at:
Didier Boursin
Boutique Setsuko et Didier
17, rue Sainte-Croix-de-la-Bretonnerie, 75004 Paris

▶ Beginner
▶▶ Intermediate
▶▶▶ Advanced

TO ALL THE CHILDREN OF ICARUS

The pilot and his crew are happy to welcome you on board this book dedicated to air and space. Our company owns a fleet consisting of 26 airplanes (gliders, delta wings) and flying objects (propeller, frisbee) ready to travel over the earth with you. We serve four destinations: traditional folds, new creations, flying objects, and collectibles. We will carry out the usual last-minute inspections before takeoff: adjustment of the wings and fitting of the ailerons and stabilizers. All the flight instructions are outlined at the beginning of the book (pages 4 to 9) in order that your time on board be as comfortable as possible. We will fly at a reasonable altitude without touching the "ceiling." We will reach our cruising speed after several hours of

practice, seated comfortably in our armchairs. We hope that you will have a pleasant and relaxing time in our company and we wish you a "bon voyage."

Introduction

Papers
The best papers are those that crease well and are sufficiently strong for repeated folding and unfolding, with a weight between 70 and 90 grams (20 to 24 lb. bond weight). Avoid papers that tear after several folds, such as certain recycled papers. White or colored papers that are used for photocopying or computer printing are excellent for folding. But investigate all the papers you have on hand: a leaflet, writing paper, or kraft paper may all do the job.

Sizes
Two sizes are commonly used to make the models in this book: small squares, and letter-sized or A4 paper. (Some models require a strip of paper, the dimensions of which are specified each time.)

Squares. For experienced folders, any size of square will work. As a rule of thumb, it's best to start big and then work down to smaller squares as you gain expertise. You may purchase square Origami paper or cut your own squares from a sheet of letter-sized or A4 paper.

Letter-sized or A4. Origami instructions often refer to A4 paper. With A4, a half or quarter of the sheet keeps the same proportions. (To get the proportion of an A4 sheet, trim ⅜ inch from the width of a letter-sized sheet.)

Adjustments

The wings of airplanes should be perfectly horizontal in flight; before launching, place them slightly above the horizontal. All the components in a model need to be checked before and after each flight: wings, ailerons and stabilizer. A badly adjusted fold will result in a mediocre flight. You also have to take humidity into account, since any moisture can make your model heavier, reducing its performance by half.

Trajectories

The quality of an airplane's flight depends on its center of gravity, that is to say, its balance. If your plane falls like a rock going into a dive, it is too heavy. You have then two solutions: lighten the front of the device, where that is possible, or else use a lighter and larger paper for folding the model.

If your plane ascends and descends by fits and starts—in other words, it stalls—it is too light in the front. To improve its flight, one or sometimes two refolds at the front will give it a better balance.

If your plane has a regular or steady trajectory, bravo! It is perfectly balanced. Certain small planes roll toward the left or right: refold the wing of each side to form ailerons; the plane should regain its stability. After several throws, experience will guide you—you'll find your flight performances improving with every launch.

Indoors or Outdoors

Most of the models are high-performance flyers indoors or outdoors. In summer and in good weather without the least wind, certain ones fly very well. For aerial demonstrations outdoors, the models with heavier noses are preferable. A light wind can also be used to improve the performance of your plane.

Throws

Certain models demand to be thrown energetically, for example, the Dart and the models that are heavier up front. Lighter models can glide very far if you accompany them with an outstretched hand. For each apparatus, it is indicated where to place your fingers for throwing. Propellers have to be held by the center with the thumb and index finger before being released. Thrown from a significant height, they need the ballast of a small stone or paper clip to give them stability,

Performance

The best performing airplanes are the simplest. They gain in aerodynamics what they lose in esthetics. More realistic-looking models will generally have reduced flight capacity. Several of these airplanes have won international competitions. All the models in this book have been tested and chosen for their excellent ability to stay in the air.

Games

All the models that you'll discover in these pages are well suited for games: organize a competition and award a prize to the airplane with the best flight time or the one that travels the greatest distance. For some people, precision is the main objective. For others, throwing a model is a way of unwinding. No matter your objective, all the foldings you put to flight will provide numerous hours of fun and relaxation.

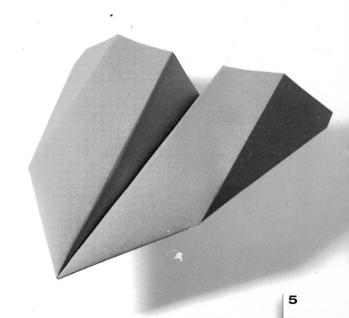

Folds and Symbols

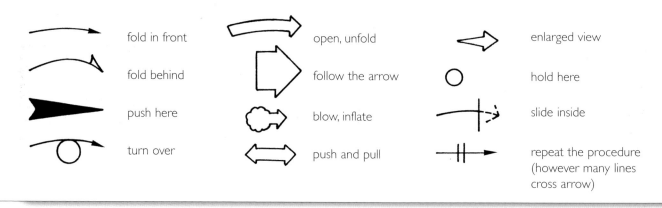

fold in front	open, unfold	enlarged view
fold behind	follow the arrow	hold here
push here	blow, inflate	slide inside
turn over	push and pull	repeat the procedure (however many lines cross arrow)

valley fold

mountain fold

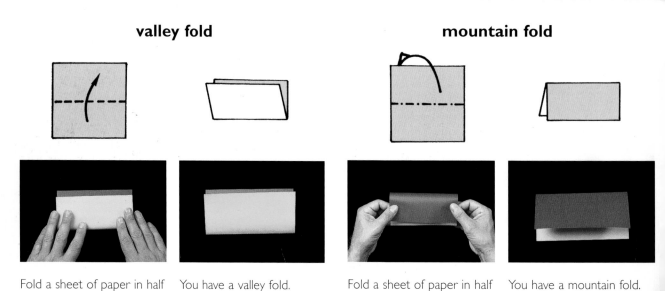

Fold a sheet of paper in half from the bottom.

You have a valley fold.

Fold a sheet of paper in half from the top.

You have a mountain fold.

crease

cut

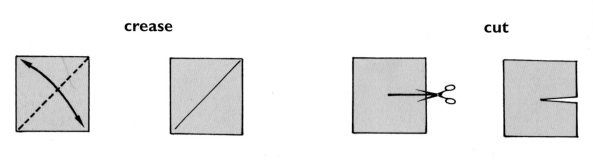

Note the difference between folding the paper and creasing (sometimes called marking the fold). When folding the paper (left square), the paper remains folded. When creasing the paper (right square), you unfold.

Preliminary Base

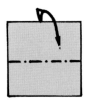

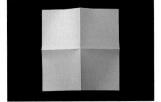
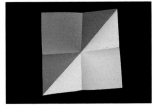
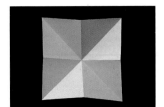

On a square sheet of paper, crease a central mountain fold.

Then crease a second central mountain fold as shown.

Crease a diagonal valley fold.

Then crease a second diagonal valley fold as shown.

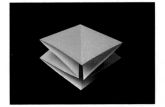

Press on the center from behind.

Grasp two opposite corners, and bring the folds together to form a diamond shape.

Flatten the entire model.

You have the preliminary base.

Matching the dots

Fold a sheet of paper from the front, as shown.

Make the fold.

Water-bomb Base

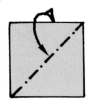
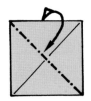

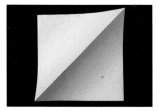

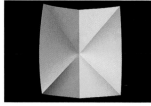
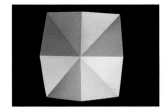

On a square sheet of paper, crease a diagonal mountain fold.

Then crease a second diagonal mountain fold as shown.

Crease a central fold in a valley fold.

Then crease a second central valley fold.

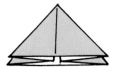

Press on the center from behind.

Grasp two opposite corners, and bring the folds together to form a triangle.

Then flatten the entire model. You have the water-bomb base.

Outside reverse fold

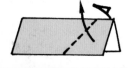

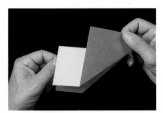

Make a valley fold, then bring the lower-right corner over as shown.

Then open.

Make the center fold a valley fold. Make mountain folds on either side of the center fold. Then push in the left side.

You have an outside reverse fold.

Inside reverse fold

  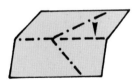 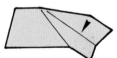

Make a valley fold, then bring the upper-right corner over as shown.

Then open.

Push down in the center to make the center fold a valley fold. Make mountain folds on either side of the center fold. Then push in the right side.

You have an inside reverse fold.

Pleat fold

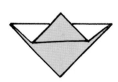

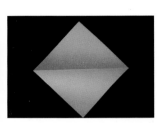  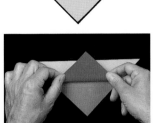 

Fold a square of paper in half from the front.

You have a triangle.

Bring up one point.

Fold again as shown. You have a pleat fold.

9

Delta Wing

▶ Beginner

This first section brings together the main traditional airplanes that everyone knows. The Delta Wing owes its originality to its nose and use of a clever locking technique. The variation on the original model is the asymmetry, which allows the model— if launched from a high place—to turn while flying.

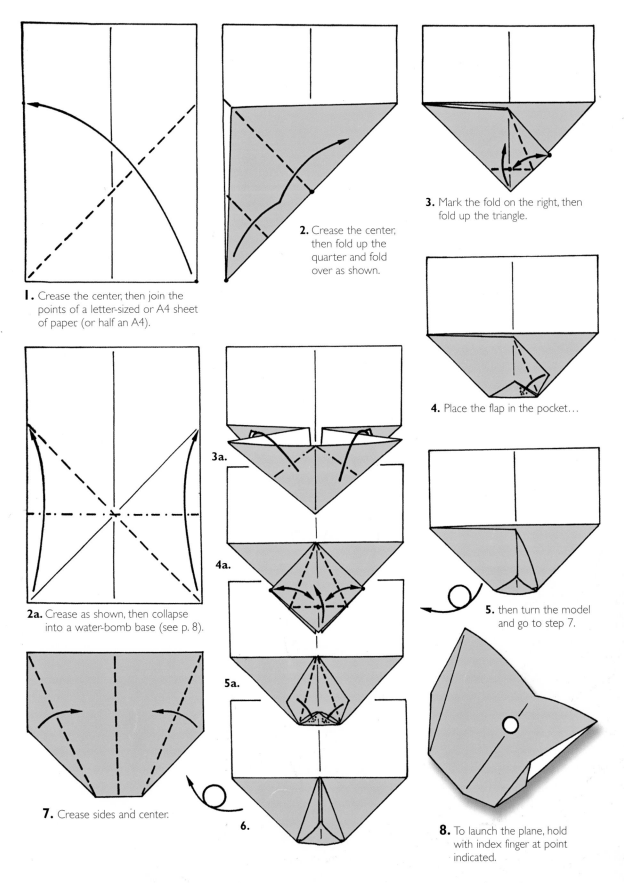

1. Crease the center, then join the points of a letter-sized or A4 sheet of paper, (or half an A4).

2. Crease the center, then fold up the quarter and fold over as shown.

3. Mark the fold on the right, then fold up the triangle.

4. Place the flap in the pocket…

2a. Crease as shown, then collapse into a water-bomb base (see p. 8).

3a.

4a.

5a.

5. then turn the model and go to step 7.

7. Crease sides and center.

6.

8. To launch the plane, hold with index finger at point indicated.

Schoolboy

▶ Beginner

Although the folding technique of this airplane is very sophisticated, it shouldn't present any difficulties. The thickness of its nose makes this plane a good outdoor flyer.

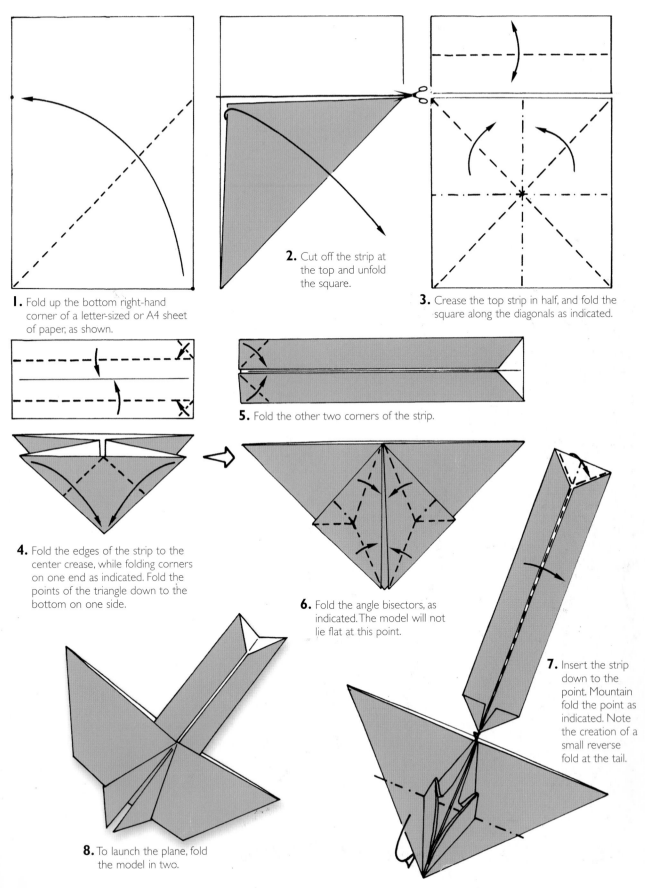

1. Fold up the bottom right-hand corner of a letter-sized or A4 sheet of paper, as shown.

2. Cut off the strip at the top and unfold the square.

3. Crease the top strip in half, and fold the square along the diagonals as indicated.

5. Fold the other two corners of the strip.

4. Fold the edges of the strip to the center crease, while folding corners on one end as indicated. Fold the points of the triangle down to the bottom on one side.

6. Fold the angle bisectors, as indicated. The model will not lie flat at this point.

7. Insert the strip down to the point. Mountain fold the point as indicated. Note the creation of a small reverse fold at the tail.

8. To launch the plane, fold the model in two.

Overflight

▶ **Beginner**

This traditional model is Japanese. You can fly this plane over unexplored territories because its wing flaps give it exceptional flight stability.

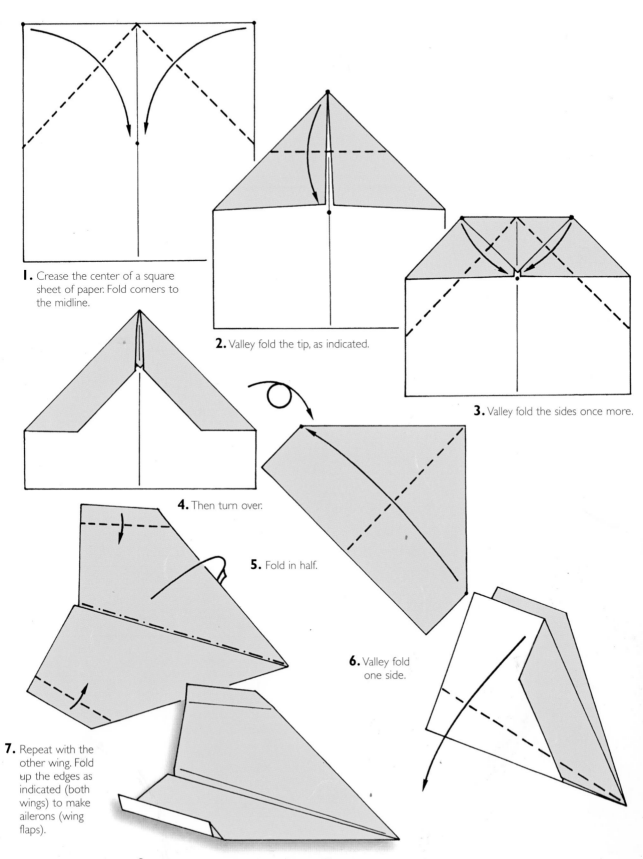

1. Crease the center of a square sheet of paper. Fold corners to the midline.

2. Valley fold the tip, as indicated.

3. Valley fold the sides once more.

4. Then turn over.

5. Fold in half.

6. Valley fold one side.

7. Repeat with the other wing. Fold up the edges as indicated (both wings) to make ailerons (wing flaps).

8. Pull up the wings, and hold from underneath to launch the plane.

Duck Plane

▶ **Beginner**

The origin of this airplane's name goes back to the beginnings of aviation. The "duck" was a plane that had its rudder in the front. It flew in 1907 with Louis Blériot at the controls. This paper version is a very capable flier.

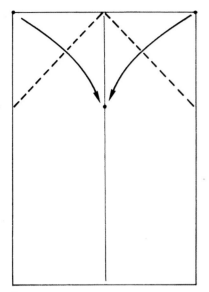

1. Crease lengthwise the center of a letter-sized or A4 sheet of paper. Fold corners to the midline…

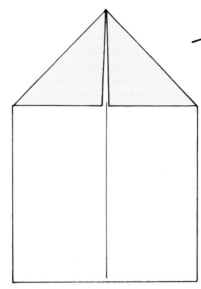

2. …like this, then turn over.

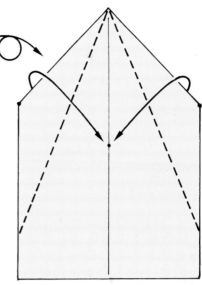

3. Fold the sides to the midline crease along the diagonal, and free the back.

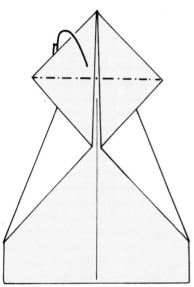

4. Mountain fold the top toward the back as shown.

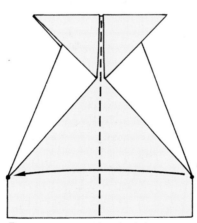

5. Valley fold in half to the left.

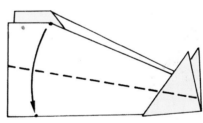

6. Fold one side down to the edge…

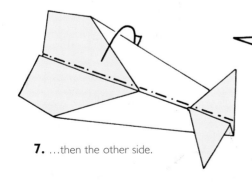

7. …then the other side.

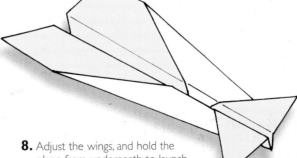

8. Adjust the wings, and hold the plane from underneath to launch.

Dart

▶ Beginner

Among the traditional paper airplanes, the Dart is the best known model because of its simple construction, combined with its excellent flight performance. It has become famous in all European playgrounds.

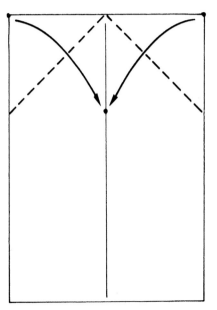

1. Crease lengthwise the center of a letter-sized or A4 sheet of paper. Fold corners to the midline.

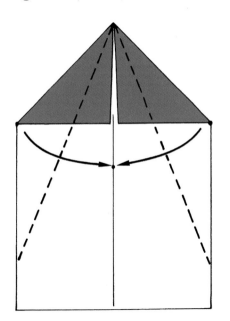

2. Fold on the diagonals to the center as shown.

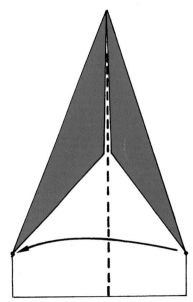

3. Fold in half.

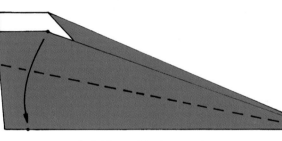

4. Fold one side down as shown…

5. …then turn it over.

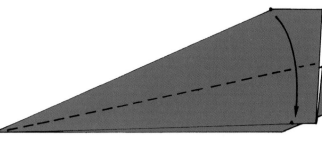

6. Fold the other side down.

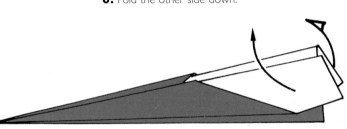

7. Bring up the sides so they will be horizontal when the Dart is in flight.

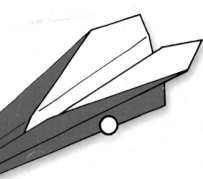

8. Hold the Dart where indicated to launch it.

Glider

▶ **Beginner**

This airplane comes from far away. Originally from China, it went from one continent to another, undergoing a few variations along the way before it arrived in Europe, where it met with unqualified success. It flies on a perfect trajectory without any premature landings. When it does come to earth, it lands softly.

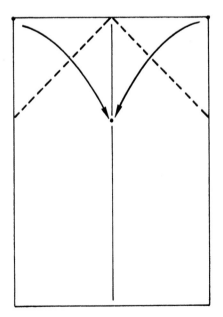

1. Crease lengthwise the center of a letter-sized or A4 sheet of paper. Fold corners to the midline.

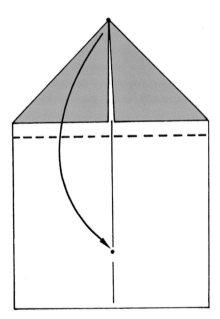

2. Valley fold the top point down onto the center line, leaving a strip as shown.

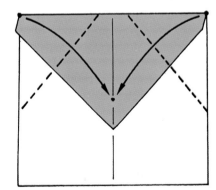

3. Then fold the points to the middle along the diagonals shown. (Folds do not meet, except at points.)

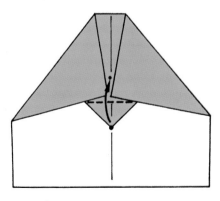

4. Valley fold the triangle up.

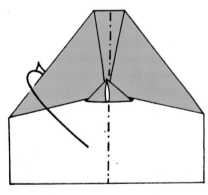

5. Mountain fold in half.

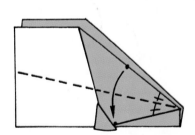

6. Fold one side down, dividing the angle in half.

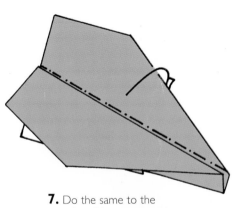

7. Do the same to the other side.

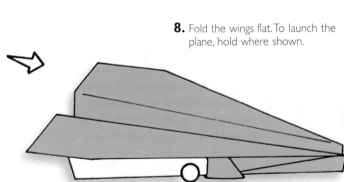

8. Fold the wings flat. To launch the plane, hold where shown.

Ready to Land

▶ **Beginner**

In this section, the paper airplanes are original contemporary creations springing from the four corners of the world. This plane flies smoothly without slipping to the ground. Although it resembles the Dart, it has a nose reinforced by several layers of paper, which allows it to fly a great distance.

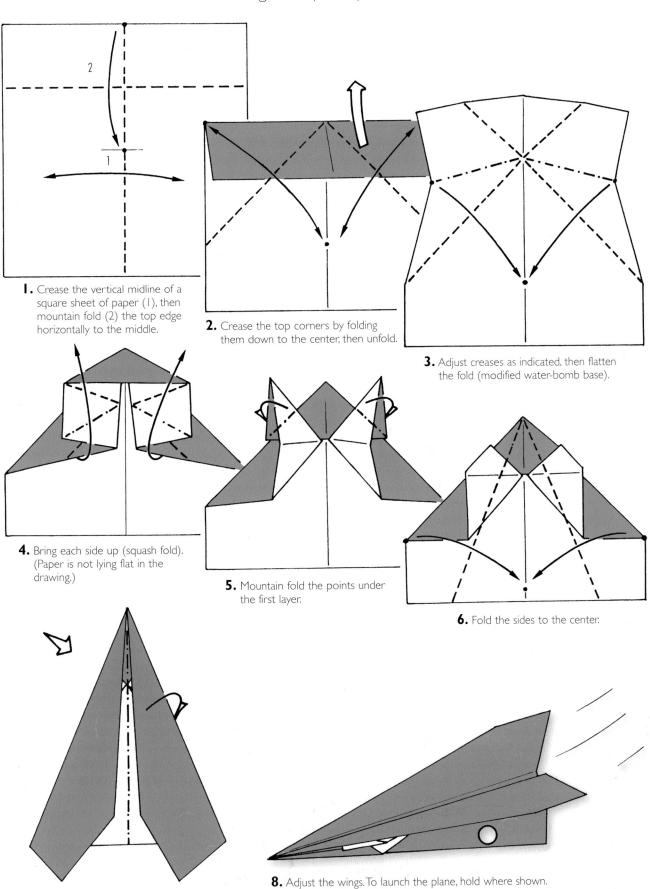

1. Crease the vertical midline of a square sheet of paper (1), then mountain fold (2) the top edge horizontally to the middle.

2. Crease the top corners by folding them down to the center, then unfold.

3. Adjust creases as indicated, then flatten the fold (modified water-bomb base).

4. Bring each side up (squash fold). (Paper is not lying flat in the drawing.)

5. Mountain fold the points under the first layer.

6. Fold the sides to the center.

7. Mountain fold in half.

8. Adjust the wings. To launch the plane, hold where shown.

Windblown

▶ Beginner

This model and its variation possess remarkable flight abilities. It will fly as easily over a classroom as over an amphitheater.

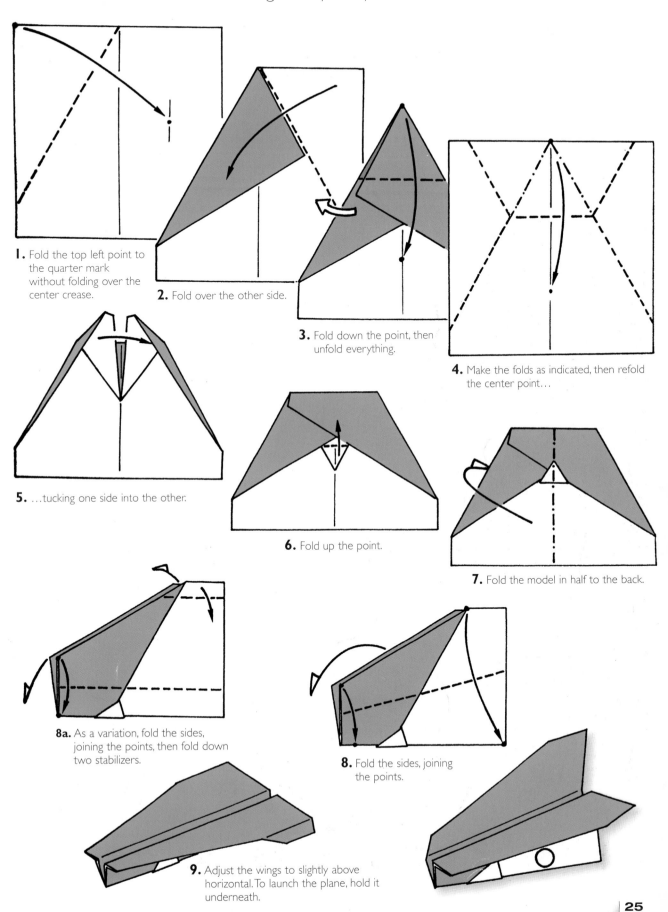

1. Fold the top left point to the quarter mark without folding over the center crease.

2. Fold over the other side.

3. Fold down the point, then unfold everything.

4. Make the folds as indicated, then refold the center point...

5. ...tucking one side into the other.

6. Fold up the point.

7. Fold the model in half to the back.

8a. As a variation, fold the sides, joining the points, then fold down two stabilizers.

8. Fold the sides, joining the points.

9. Adjust the wings to slightly above horizontal. To launch the plane, hold it underneath.

Uranus Arc II

▶ Beginner

This airplane won a competition during an exhibition at the Air and Space
Museum at the Bourget Airport. Nicolas Beaudiez, the creator, relied on the
aerodynamics of the nose and wings to give the best possible performance.
The plane should be launched from a high point.

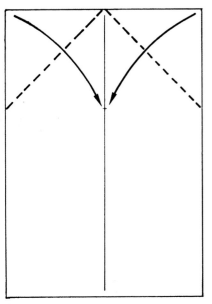

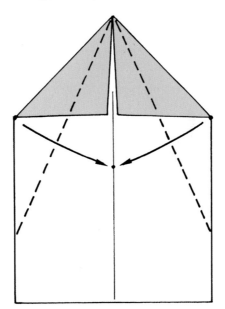

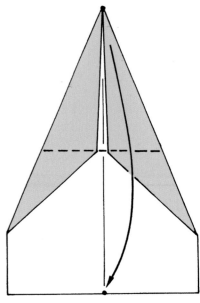

1. Crease lengthwise the center of a letter-sized or A4 sheet of paper. Fold top corners to the midline.

2. Fold the corners to the center again.

3. Valley fold the model in half, and turn over.

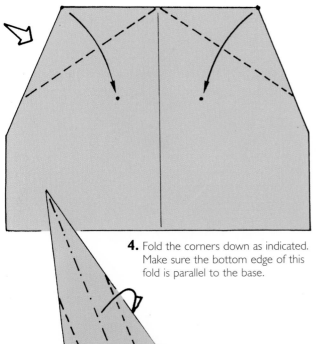

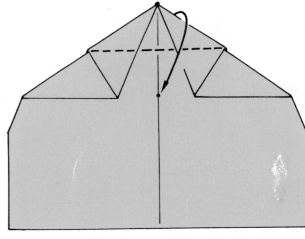

4. Fold the corners down as indicated. Make sure the bottom edge of this fold is parallel to the base.

5. Mountain fold as indicated, allowing the long point to flip out from the back.

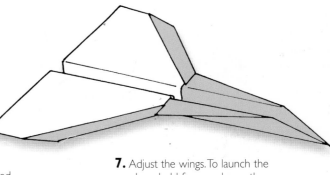

6. Crease twice as indicated on each side of the midline, then fold in half.

7. Adjust the wings. To launch the plane, hold from underneath.

Nonstop

▶ Beginner

This model is Japanese and was created by Takeshi Inoué. It's a boomerang plane that, once thrown, returns to its departure point after making a large loop. The game consists of catching it in the palm of your hand without letting it touch the ground.

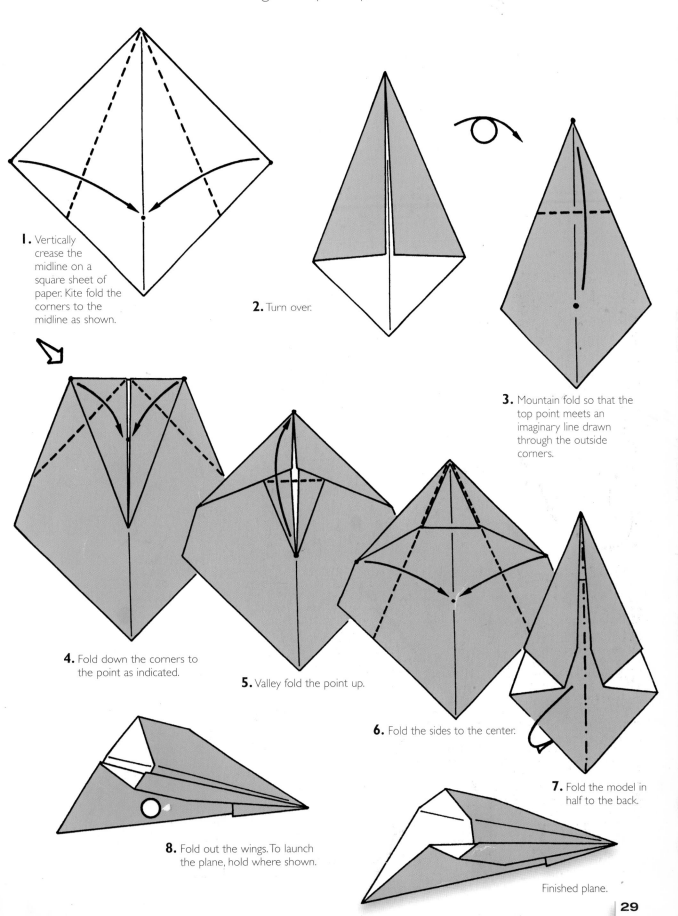

1. Vertically crease the midline on a square sheet of paper. Kite fold the corners to the midline as shown.

2. Turn over.

3. Mountain fold so that the top point meets an imaginary line drawn through the outside corners.

4. Fold down the corners to the point as indicated.

5. Valley fold the point up.

6. Fold the sides to the center.

7. Fold the model in half to the back.

8. Fold out the wings. To launch the plane, hold where shown.

Finished plane.

Ready for Takeoff

▶ Beginner

The large wings on this model give it a slow and stable flight. It is remarkably simple to fold.

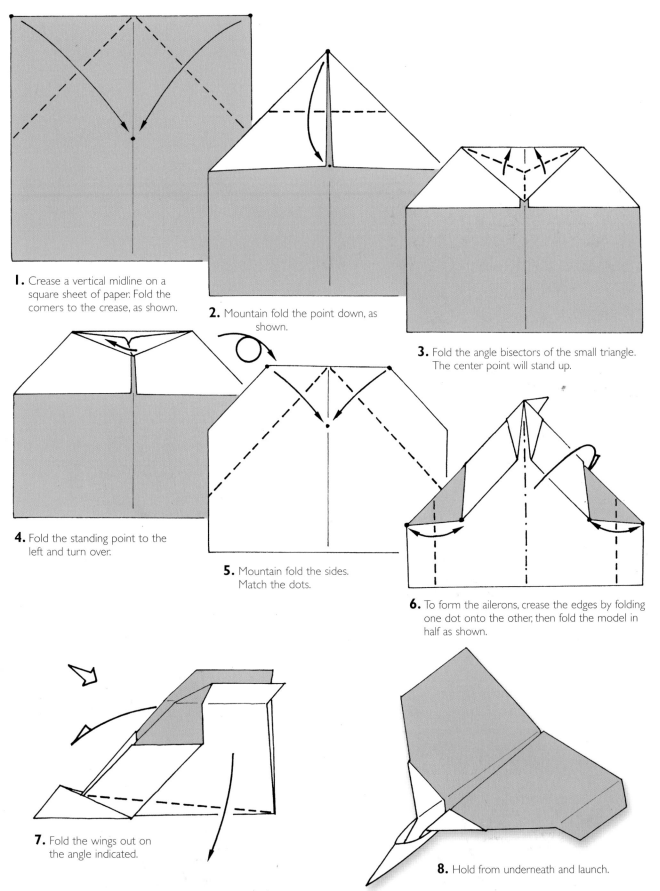

1. Crease a vertical midline on a square sheet of paper. Fold the corners to the crease, as shown.

2. Mountain fold the point down, as shown.

3. Fold the angle bisectors of the small triangle. The center point will stand up.

4. Fold the standing point to the left and turn over.

5. Mountain fold the sides. Match the dots.

6. To form the ailerons, crease the edges by folding one dot onto the other, then fold the model in half as shown.

7. Fold the wings out on the angle indicated.

8. Hold from underneath and launch.

Looping

▶▶ Intermediate

This contemporary model is made from a small square of paper. If you stretch out your arm when you throw it, it will delight you with a series of aerial acrobatics before landing a few yards away.

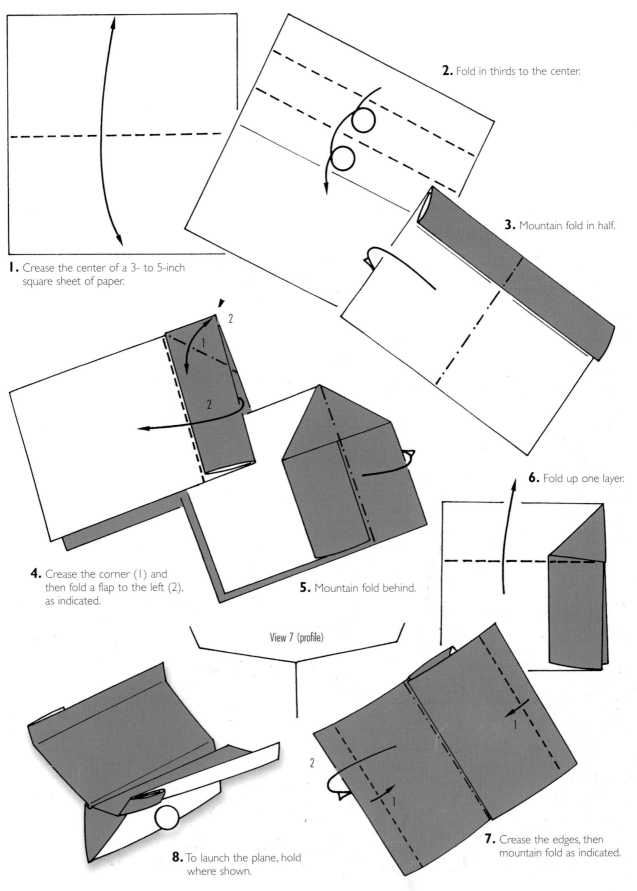

1. Crease the center of a 3- to 5-inch square sheet of paper.

2. Fold in thirds to the center.

3. Mountain fold in half.

4. Crease the corner (1) and then fold a flap to the left (2), as indicated.

5. Mountain fold behind.

6. Fold up one layer.

View 7 (profile)

7. Crease the edges, then mountain fold as indicated.

8. To launch the plane, hold where shown.

33

Gliding Flight

▶▶ **Intermediate**

This model takes advantage of the perfect geometric proportions of A4 size paper. (Trim ⅝ inch from the width of a letter-sized sheet.) The plane is sufficiently heavy to fly outdoors. Its shape, with the back aileron sticking up, allows it to fly a good distance away and for a long time.

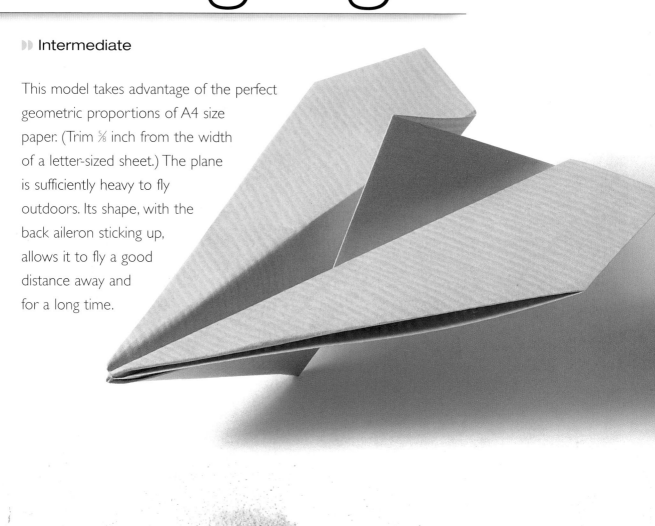

1. Crease lengthwise the center of a sheet of A4 paper. Fold corners to the midline.

2. Then turn over.

3. Fold the sides to the center, and free the back…

4. …like this, then turn over.

5. Mountain fold as indicated.

6. Lift the point.

7. Fold as indicated, and insert the corners into the pockets.

8. Fold the sides to the center (1), then fold in half to the rear (2).

9. At this stage, the model flies well. You could bring up the back aileron by creasing the diagonal…

10. …then making an inside reverse fold (see p. 8).

11. To launch the plane, hold where shown.

Imaginary Voyage

▶▶ Intermediate   In our dreams, we often fly over imaginary lands. This little airplane will allow us to travel in spirit as if in a fairy tale.

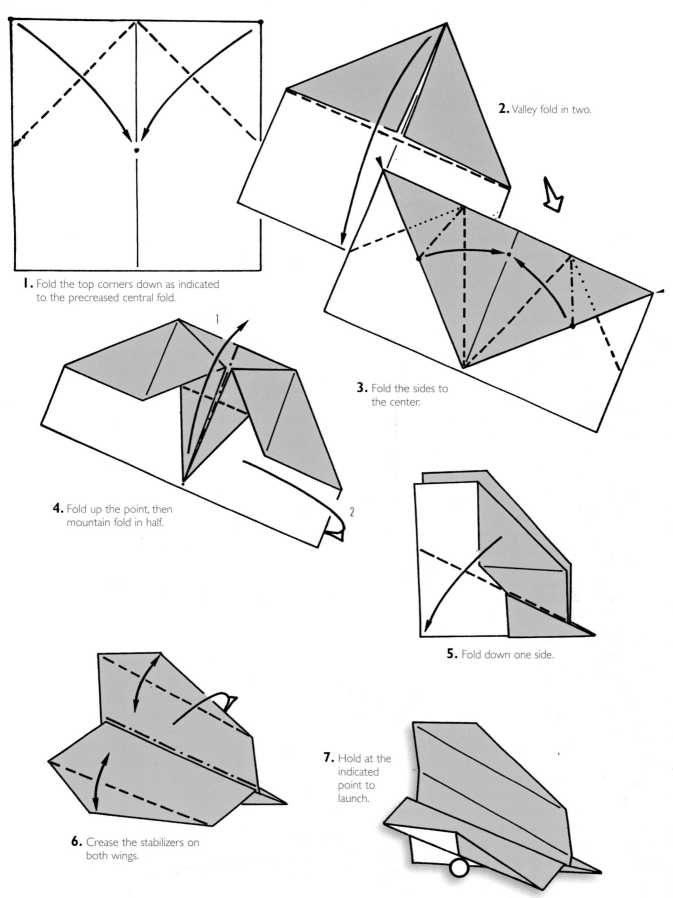

1. Fold the top corners down as indicated to the precreased central fold.

2. Valley fold in two.

3. Fold the sides to the center.

4. Fold up the point, then mountain fold in half.

5. Fold down one side.

6. Crease the stabilizers on both wings.

7. Hold at the indicated point to launch.

Stealth

>>> **Advanced**

Stephen Weiss created this model, which he called
Level Track Delta. The elegant design with its
swept-back wings
gives this plane
perfect
stability.

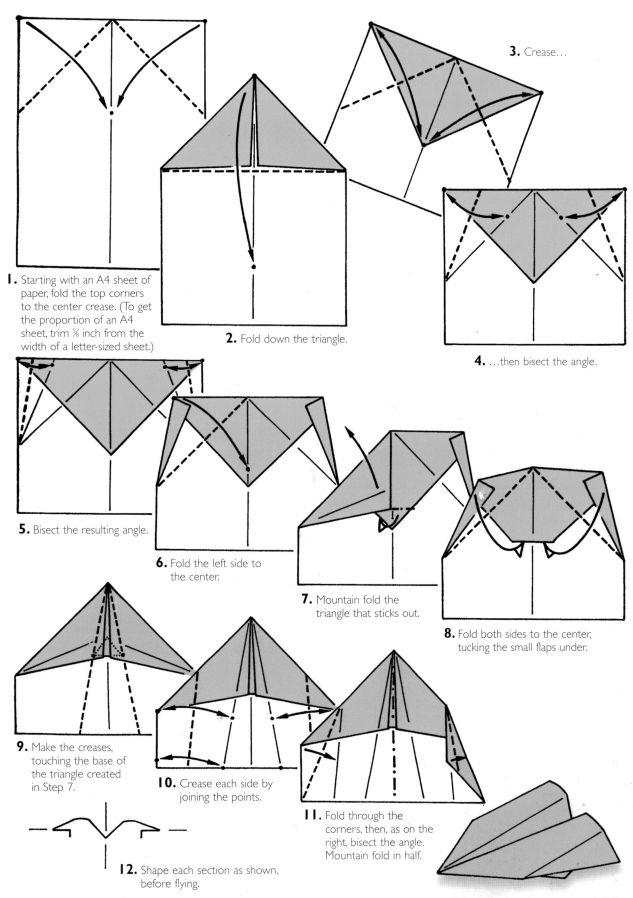

1. Starting with an A4 sheet of paper, fold the top corners to the center crease. (To get the proportion of an A4 sheet, trim ⅜ inch from the width of a letter-sized sheet.)

2. Fold down the triangle.

3. Crease…

4. …then bisect the angle.

5. Bisect the resulting angle.

6. Fold the left side to the center.

7. Mountain fold the triangle that sticks out.

8. Fold both sides to the center, tucking the small flaps under.

9. Make the creases, touching the base of the triangle created in Step 7.

10. Crease each side by joining the points.

11. Fold through the corners, then, as on the right, bisect the angle. Mountain fold in half.

12. Shape each section as shown, before flying.

Windflight

▶ Beginner

Although this little airplane is simple to fold, it glides remarkably well. To help its flight, stretch out your arm when you throw it.

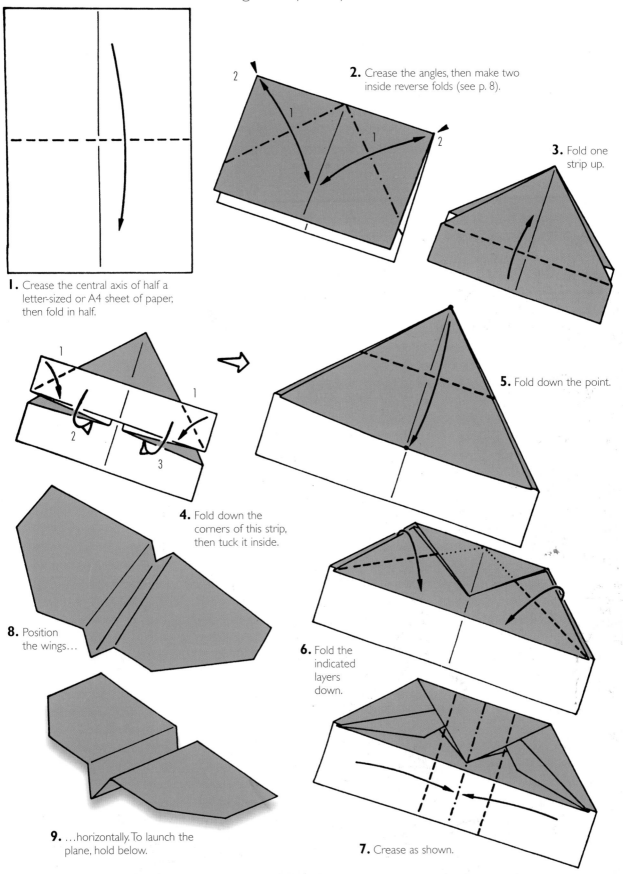

1. Crease the central axis of half a letter-sized or A4 sheet of paper, then fold in half.

2. Crease the angles, then make two inside reverse folds (see p. 8).

3. Fold one strip up.

4. Fold down the corners of this strip, then tuck it inside.

5. Fold down the point.

6. Fold the indicated layers down.

7. Crease as shown.

8. Position the wings…

9. …horizontally. To launch the plane, hold below.

Tube and Paper Twirler

▶ **Beginner**

This section gathers together some flying paper-foldings that are not airplanes. The tube, thrown sharply out of a window away from the wall toward the horizon, will fly for about 30 feet, landing softly in the street on the opposite side. The paper twirler is simple to make, but will amaze you when you drop it from a high place: it will spin around itself as it falls.

Tube

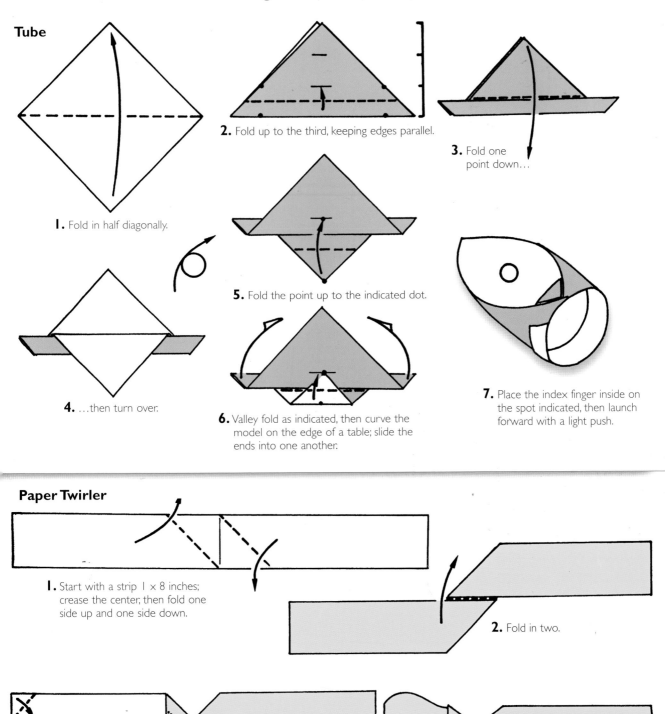

1. Fold in half diagonally.

2. Fold up to the third, keeping edges parallel.

3. Fold one point down…

4. …then turn over.

5. Fold the point up to the indicated dot.

6. Valley fold as indicated, then curve the model on the edge of a table; slide the ends into one another.

7. Place the index finger inside on the spot indicated, then launch forward with a light push.

Paper Twirler

1. Start with a strip 1 x 8 inches; crease the center, then fold one side up and one side down.

2. Fold in two.

3. Fold in the corners of the left side, then slide it into the pocket of the center triangle…

4. …like this, then turn over.

5. Fold the corners of the right side the same way.

6. Crease the middle; hold the model vertically at the spot shown. Let go and it will fall, turning on itself.

Rotor

▶ Beginner

This twin-blade model will turn in either direction, depending on how the first folds were made. The name "Rotor" was chosen for a similar reason: it is the same spelled forward or backward.

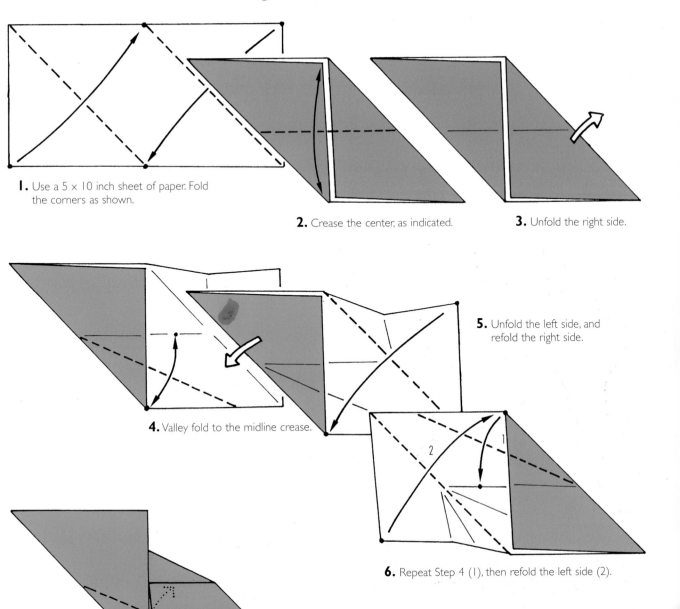

1. Use a 5 x 10 inch sheet of paper. Fold the corners as shown.

2. Crease the center, as indicated.

3. Unfold the right side.

4. Valley fold to the midline crease.

5. Unfold the left side, and refold the right side.

6. Repeat Step 4 (1), then refold the left side (2).

7. Refold on existing crease, while tucking under flap.

8. Fold each side in half. (Folds continue under flaps.)

9. Hold the model in the middle between your thumb and index finger. Then release it, letting it spiral slowly to the ground.

Propeller

Philip Shen created the propeller on which this model is based. You'll find the model extremely simple to make. You may pin it to a dowel or a piece of wood, tacking the head down from the inside in the center of the propeller. When you move the dowel, the propeller will turn with the whir of a motor.

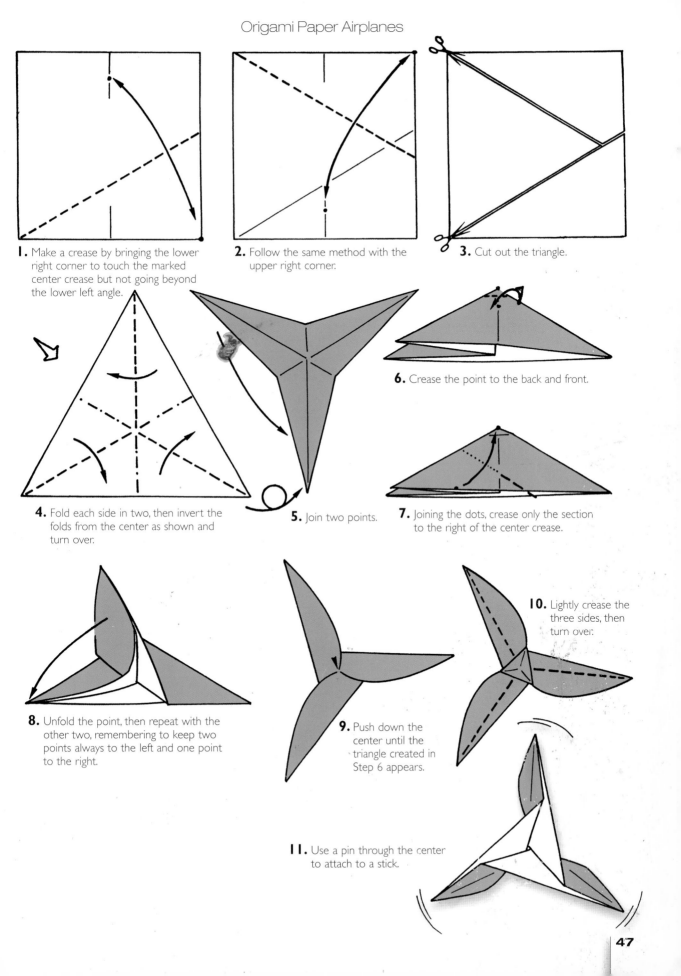

1. Make a crease by bringing the lower right corner to touch the marked center crease but not going beyond the lower left angle.

2. Follow the same method with the upper right corner.

3. Cut out the triangle.

4. Fold each side in two, then invert the folds from the center as shown and turn over.

5. Join two points.

6. Crease the point to the back and front.

7. Joining the dots, crease only the section to the right of the center crease.

8. Unfold the point, then repeat with the other two, remembering to keep two points always to the left and one point to the right.

9. Push down the center until the triangle created in Step 6 appears.

10. Lightly crease the three sides, then turn over.

11. Use a pin through the center to attach to a stick.

Frisbee

▶▶ Intermediate

A frisbee needs two people to play so both players should get involved in constructing the eight elements that make up this paper frisbee. As it is a very light model, it can only be used indoors.

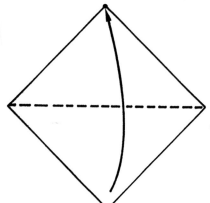

1. Fold in two.

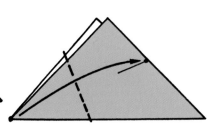

2. Mark the right side by bisecting the angle on the left of the top layer only.

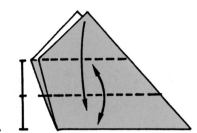

3. Fold the point to the mark.

4. Crease through all thicknesses.

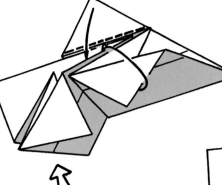

5. Unfold the point, then fold in while opening slightly (see p. 9, inside reverse fold).

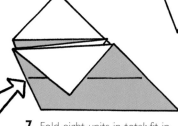

6. Crease the half as shown, then fold down one point.

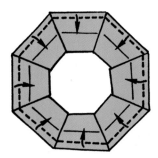

7. Fold eight units in total; fit in another section by the point…

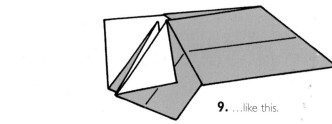

8. …then, place one unit at a time inside the last, folding the triangles in front and behind inside to lock the assembly…

9. …like this.

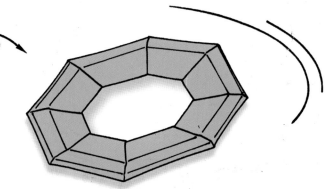

10. With the ring finished, crease a narrow border around it, then turn over.

11. The frisbee is ready to be thrown.

Silent Spinner

❱❱ Intermediate

This propeller is a modified traditional model. These three strips woven together will come alive with a rustling of paper when you put them on the tip of a pencil and whirl it around.

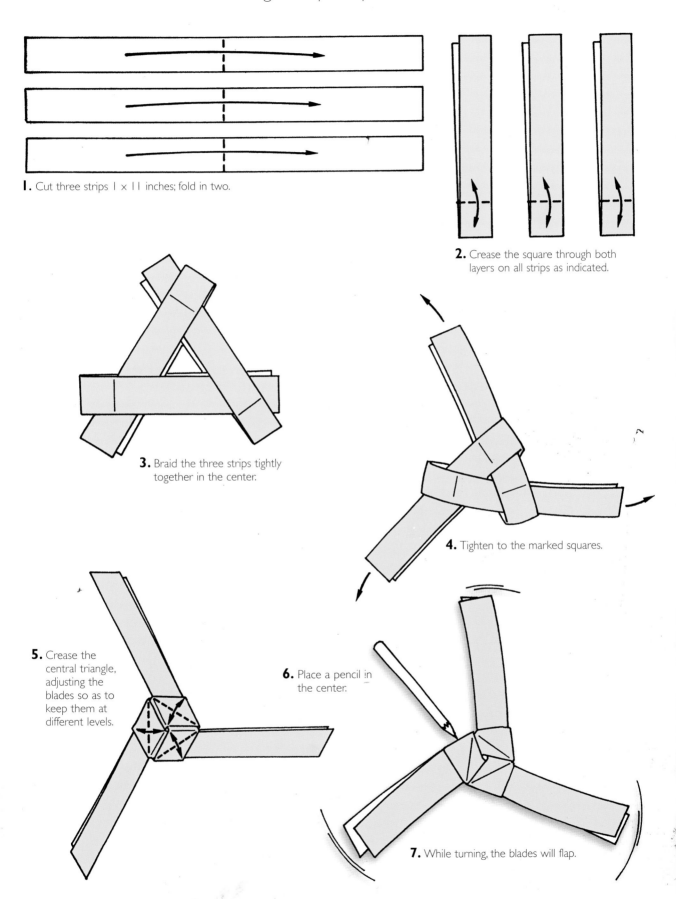

1. Cut three strips 1 x 11 inches; fold in two.

2. Crease the square through both layers on all strips as indicated.

3. Braid the three strips tightly together in the center.

4. Tighten to the marked squares.

5. Crease the central triangle, adjusting the blades so as to keep them at different levels.

6. Place a pencil in the center.

7. While turning, the blades will flap.

Windmill

Thrown from a certain height, this model will turn at an ever increasing speed because its bent blades scoop up air during the fall. You can also place it on a thin wire or thread and it will twirl as the wind blows.

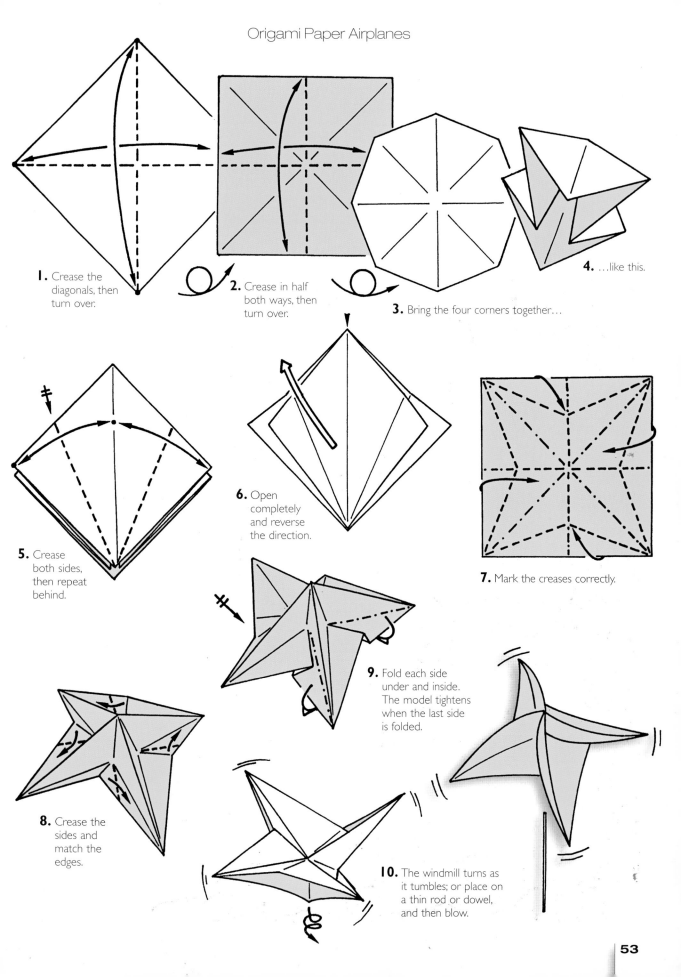

1. Crease the diagonals, then turn over.

2. Crease in half both ways, then turn over.

3. Bring the four corners together…

4. …like this.

5. Crease both sides, then repeat behind.

6. Open completely and reverse the direction.

7. Mark the creases correctly.

8. Crease the sides and match the edges.

9. Fold each side under and inside. The model tightens when the last side is folded.

10. The windmill turns as it tumbles; or place on a thin rod or dowel, and then blow.

Chopper

▶ **Beginner**

Antoine de Saint-Exupéry, author
of *The Little Prince*, loved
to fold
helicopters like
this one when he
was between flights. He
would hurl them out of
windows to the great delight of
children. This model returns to the
principle of the original folds.

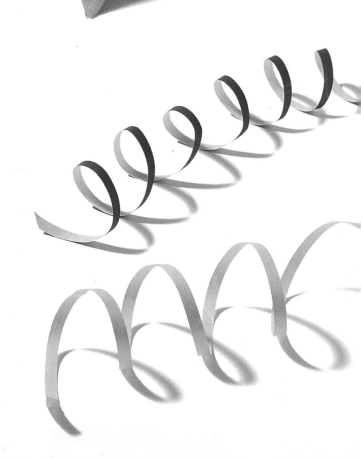

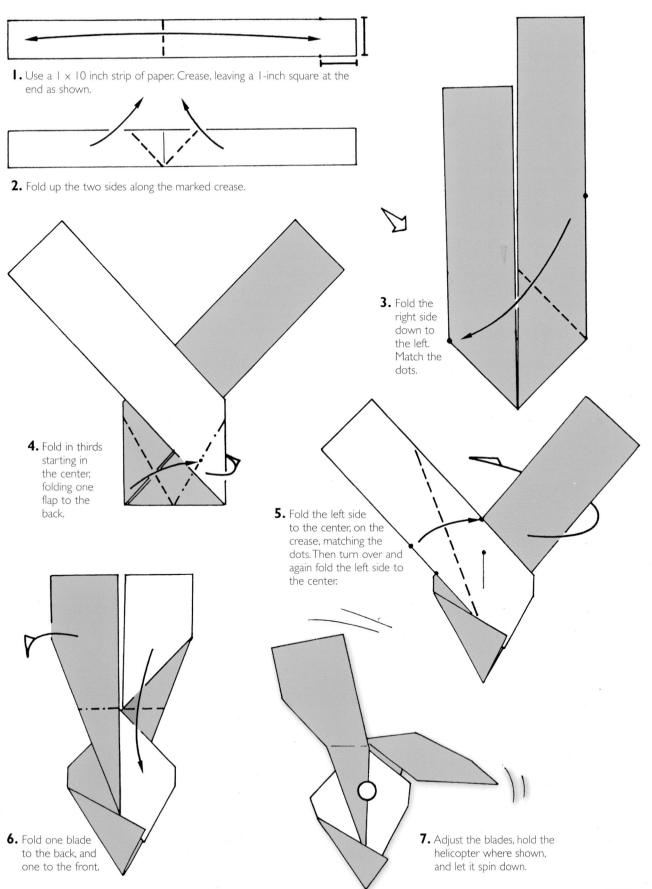

1. Use a 1 x 10 inch strip of paper. Crease, leaving a 1-inch square at the end as shown.

2. Fold up the two sides along the marked crease.

3. Fold the right side down to the left. Match the dots.

4. Fold in thirds starting in the center, folding one flap to the back.

5. Fold the left side to the center, on the crease, matching the dots. Then turn over and again fold the left side to the center.

6. Fold one blade to the back, and one to the front.

7. Adjust the blades, hold the helicopter where shown, and let it spin down.

Connecting Flight

>> Intermediate

The models presented in this section don't fly. They are like objects in any collection that are simply to be admired and placed on bookshelves. This model is the improved version of a prototype created by Michel Roy a few years ago. This little plane is dedicated to all the urban travelers who keep their feet on the ground. Why not pin it to the lapel of your jacket?

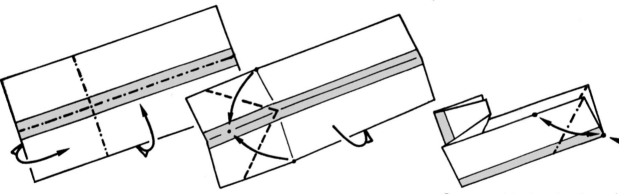

1. Start with a rectangle, with proportions of 1:2. Crease at one-third of the length and also lengthwise at the center.

2. Align these creases as shown, creating a valley fold in the process.

3. Crease, joining the points, then make a reverse fold (see pages 8 and 9).

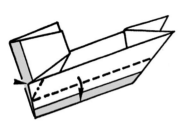

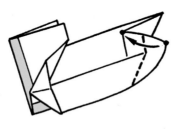

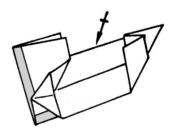

4. Fold the edge in two, making a squash fold on the left side.

5. Fold up the right side, joining the points.

6. Repeat Steps 4 and 5 on the other side, then turn over.

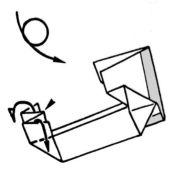

8. Holding where indicated, flatten the wings while aligning the center folds…

7. Open each side of the tail, flattening the center fold.

9. …like this

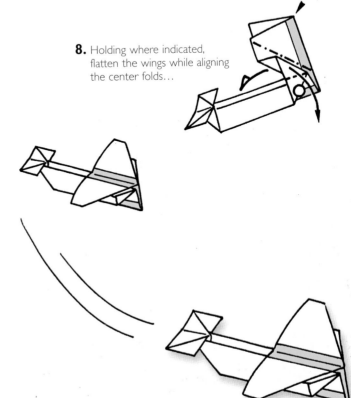

Squadron

▶▶ Intermediate

This model reminds one of the folding technique used in Schoolboy, which was explained in the first section. It's a traditional Chinese model. Assembling a couple of small airplanes on top of the big one produces an overall effect of power to the whole group.

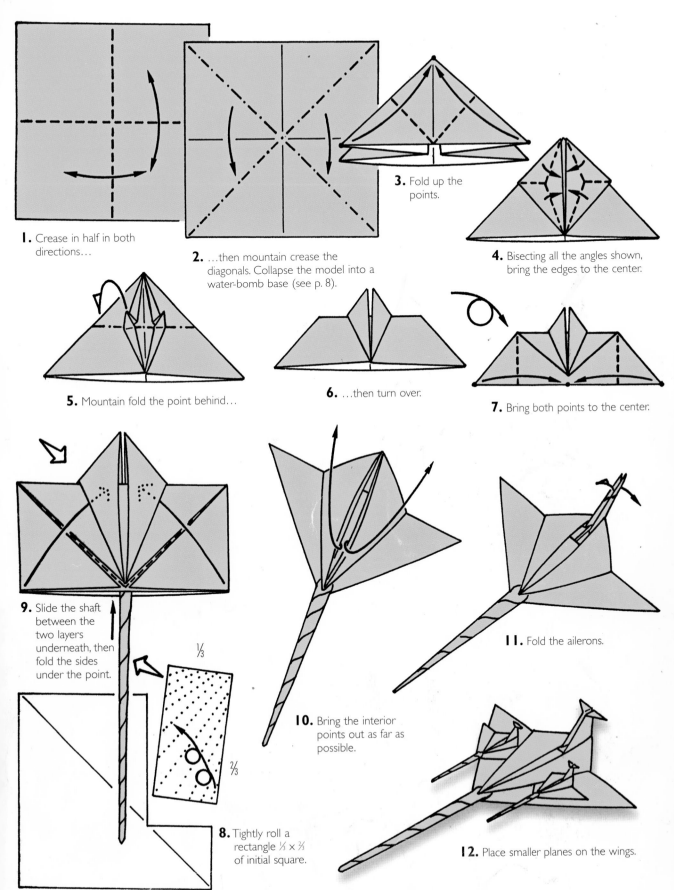

1. Crease in half in both directions…

2. …then mountain crease the diagonals. Collapse the model into a water-bomb base (see p. 8).

3. Fold up the points.

4. Bisecting all the angles shown, bring the edges to the center.

5. Mountain fold the point behind…

6. …then turn over.

7. Bring both points to the center.

9. Slide the shaft between the two layers underneath, then fold the sides under the point.

⅓

⅔

8. Tightly roll a rectangle ⅓ × ⅔ of initial square.

10. Bring the interior points out as far as possible.

11. Fold the ailerons.

12. Place smaller planes on the wings.

Sound Barrier

▶▶ Intermediate

This paper-folding was designed to go along naturally with the proportions of an A4 piece of paper. It proceeds in logical steps of folding and results in this esthetically beautiful plane. (To get the proportion of an A4 sheet, trim ⅝ inch from the width of a letter-sized sheet.)

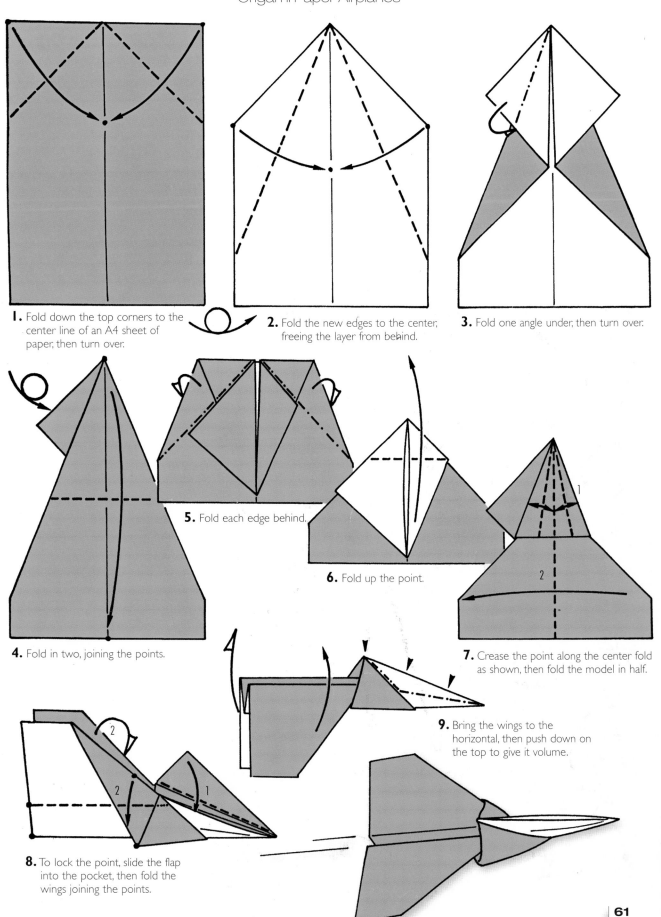

1. Fold down the top corners to the center line of an A4 sheet of paper, then turn over.

2. Fold the new edges to the center, freeing the layer from behind.

3. Fold one angle under, then turn over.

5. Fold each edge behind.

6. Fold up the point.

4. Fold in two, joining the points.

7. Crease the point along the center fold as shown, then fold the model in half.

9. Bring the wings to the horizontal, then push down on the top to give it volume.

8. To lock the point, slide the flap into the pocket, then fold the wings joining the points.

Designs

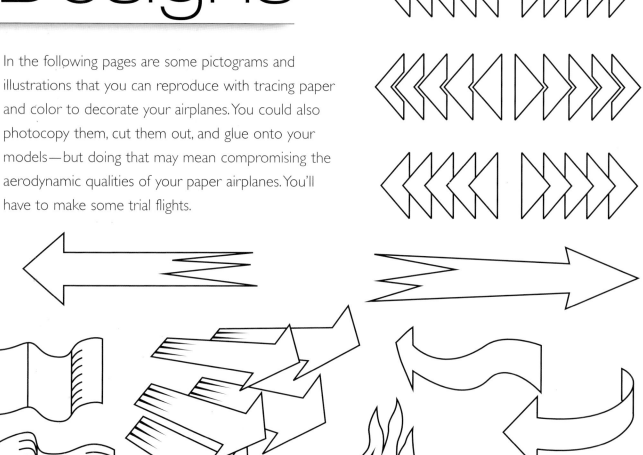

In the following pages are some pictograms and illustrations that you can reproduce with tracing paper and color to decorate your airplanes. You could also photocopy them, cut them out, and glue onto your models—but doing that may mean compromising the aerodynamic qualities of your paper airplanes. You'll have to make some trial flights.

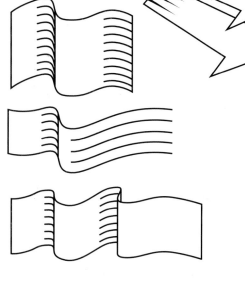

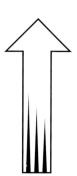

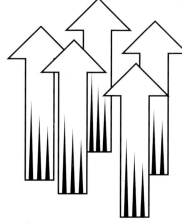

Here are some examples in color for you to decorate your planes.